Pray, Sing, Worship

Originally published in Australia in 2000 by the General Synod of the Anglican Church of Australia under the imprint Broughton Books as *Singing and Praying Together: A Communion Book for Young People from A Prayer Book for Australia*

Published in Australia in 2011 by Broughton Publishing Pty Ltd, www.broughtonpublishing.com.au, as *My Illustrated Prayer Book*

First published in Great Britain in 2011

Society for Promoting Christian Knowledge
36 Causton Street
London SW1P 4ST
www.spckpublishing.co.uk

British Library Cataloguing-in-Publication Data
A catalogue record for this book is available from the British Library

ISBN 978–0–281–06590–5 (pbk)
ISBN 978–0–281–06591–2 (hbk)

10 9 8 7 6 5 4 3 2 1

Printed in China by New Era Printing Company

Pray, Sing, Worship

A picture book for Holy Communion

The Gathering

The Greeting

A minister greets us:
The Lord be with you

We say:
and also with you.

Prayer of Preparation

We get ready to worship God:
Almighty God,
to whom all hearts are open,
all desires known,
and from whom no secrets are hidden:
cleanse the thoughts of our hearts
by the inspiration of your Holy Spirit,
that we may perfectly love you,
and worthily magnify your holy name;
through Christ our Lord.
Amen.

Prayers of Penitence

We say sorry to God for the things we have done wrong:
Most merciful God,
Father of our Lord Jesus Christ,
we confess that we have sinned
in thought, word and deed.
We have not loved you with our whole heart.
We have not loved our neighbours as ourselves.
In your mercy
forgive what we have been,
help us to amend what we are,
and direct what we shall be;
that we may do justly,
love mercy,
and walk humbly with you, our God.
Amen.

A priest says:
Almighty God,
who forgives all who truly repent,
have mercy upon *you*,
pardon and deliver *you* from all *your* sins,
confirm and strengthen *you* in all goodness,
and keep *you* in life eternal;
through Jesus Christ our Lord.

We say:
Amen.

Gloria in Excelsis

We praise God by saying or singing:
Glory to God in the highest,
and peace to his people on earth.

Lord God, heavenly King,
almighty God and Father,
we worship you, we give you thanks,
we praise you for your glory.

Lord Jesus Christ, only Son of the Father,
Lord God, Lamb of God,
you take away the sin of the world:
have mercy on us;
you are seated at the right hand of the Father:
receive our prayer.

For you alone are the Holy One,
you alone are the Lord,
you alone are the Most High, Jesus Christ,
with the Holy Spirit,
in the glory of God the Father.
Amen.

The Collect

*The prayer for today
is said.*

We say:
Amen.

The Liturgy of the Word

We listen to readings from the Bible.

Readings

At the end of the readings, the reader says:
This is the word of the Lord.

We say:
Thanks be to God.

Gospel Reading

The reader says:
Hear the Gospel of our Lord Jesus Christ according to . . . .

We say:
Glory to you, O Lord.

At the end of the reading, the reader says:
This is the Gospel of the Lord.

We say:
Praise to you, O Christ.

Sermon

We hear more about the Bible readings.

The Creed

We join together to say what the Church believes:
We believe in one God,
the Father, the Almighty,
maker of heaven and earth,
of all that is,
seen and unseen.

We believe in one Lord, Jesus Christ,
the only Son of God,
eternally begotten of the Father,
God from God, Light from Light,
true God from true God,
begotten, not made,
of one Being with the Father;
through him all things were made.
For us and for our salvation he came down from heaven,
was incarnate from the Holy Spirit and the Virgin Mary
and was made man.
For our sake he was crucified under Pontius Pilate;
he suffered death and was buried . . .

On the third day he rose again
in accordance with the Scriptures;
he ascended into heaven
and is seated at the right hand of the Father.
He will come again in glory to judge the living and the dead,
and his kingdom will have no end.

We believe in the Holy Spirit,
the Lord, the giver of life,
who proceeds from the Father and the Son,
who with the Father and the Son is worshipped and glorified,
who has spoken through the prophets.
We believe in one holy catholic and apostolic Church.
We acknowledge one baptism for the forgiveness of sins.
We look for the resurrection of the dead,
and the life of the world to come.
Amen.

13

Prayers of Intercession

We ask God to look after all who need his help.

After each prayer, the reader may say:
Lord, in your mercy

We say:
hear our prayer.

At the end of the prayers, the reader may say:
Merciful Father,

We say:
accept these prayers
for the sake of your Son,
our Saviour Jesus Christ.
Amen.

The Liturgy of the Sacrament

The Peace

The minister says:
The peace of the Lord be always with you

We say:
and also with you.

The priest may say:
Let us offer one another a sign of peace.

We share a sign of peace.

Preparation of the Table

The bread and wine are placed on the table.

The priest may say a prayer:
Blessed are you, Lord God of all creation:
through your goodness we have this bread to set before you,
which earth has given and human hands have made.
It will become for us the bread of life.

We say:
Blessed be God for ever.

The priest may say:
Blessed are you, Lord God of all creation:
through your goodness we have this wine to set before you,
fruit of the vine and work of human hands.
It will become for us the cup of salvation.

We say:
Blessed be God for ever.

The Eucharistic Prayer

The priest says:
The Lord be with you

We say:
and also with you.

Lift up your hearts.

We lift them to the Lord.

Let us give thanks to the Lord our God.

It is right to give thanks and praise.

During the prayer,
we say or sing:
Holy, holy, holy Lord,
God of power and might,
heaven and earth are full of your glory.
Hosanna in the highest.
Blessed is he who comes in the name of the Lord.
Hosanna in the highest.

Christ has died:
Christ is risen:
Christ will come again.

At the end, we may say or sing:
Blessing and honour and glory and power
be yours for ever and ever.
Amen.

The Lord's Prayer

We say the prayer that Jesus taught us:
Our Father in heaven,
hallowed be your name,
your kingdom come,
your will be done,
on earth as in heaven.
Give us today our daily bread.
Forgive us our sins
as we forgive those who sin against us.
Lead us not into temptation
but deliver us from evil.
For the kingdom, the power,
and the glory are yours
now and for ever.
Amen.

Breaking of the Bread

The priest says:
We break this bread
to share in the body of Christ.

We all say:
Though we are many, we are one body,
because we all share in one bread.

The priest invites us to Communion:
Draw near with faith.
Receive the body of our Lord Jesus Christ
which he gave for you,
and his blood which he shed for you.
Eat and drink
in remembrance that he died for you,
and feed on him in your hearts
by faith with thanksgiving.

Giving of Communion

We receive Holy Communion or a blessing.

The priest may say:
The body of Christ keep you in eternal life.

We say:
Amen.

The blood of Christ keep
you in eternal life.

Amen.

Prayer after Communion

We may say this prayer:
Almighty God,
we thank you for feeding us
with the body and blood of your Son Jesus Christ.
Through him we offer you our souls and bodies
to be a living sacrifice.
Send us out
in the power of your Spirit
to live and work
to your praise and glory.
Amen.

29

The Dismissal

The priest prays for God to bless us all:
. . . the blessing of God almighty,
the Father, the Son, and the Holy Spirit,
be among you and remain with you always.

We say:
Amen.

*A minister sends us out to live for God
during the week:*
Go in peace to love and serve the Lord.

We say:
In the name of Christ. Amen.

ND - #0060 - 270325 - C32 - 220/210/2 - PB - 9780281065905 - Gloss Lamination